Lunar New Year
A Celebration of Family and Fun

By Mary Man-Kong

Illustrated by Michelle Jing Chan

🌑 A GOLDEN BOOK • NEW YORK

rhcbooks.com
Educators and librarians, for a variety of teaching tools, visit us at RHTeachersLibrarians.com
Library of Congress Control Number: 2022942314
ISBN 978-0-593-64946-6 (trade) — ISBN 978-0-593-64947-3 (ebook)
Printed in the United States of America
10 9 8 7 6 5 4 3 2 1

It's time to celebrate the Lunar New Year!
Grandparents, parents, and children all
come together to join in the fun.

The New Year begins when the first new moon of the lunar calendar is in the sky. Celebrations last for fifteen days and end when the moon is full.

More than 1.5 billion people enjoy Lunar New Year festivities! It is celebrated in different countries in Asia and in countries where a lot of Asian families live.

China

Xīn nián kuài lè!

Saehae bok mani badeuseyo!

Korea

There are many ways to wish someone a happy New Year:

Thailand

Sùk săn wan dtrùt jeen!

Vietnam

Chúc Mừng Năm Mới!

Every Lunar New Year is named for one of the twelve zodiac animals: rat, ox, tiger, rabbit, dragon, snake, horse, goat, monkey, rooster, dog, and pig.

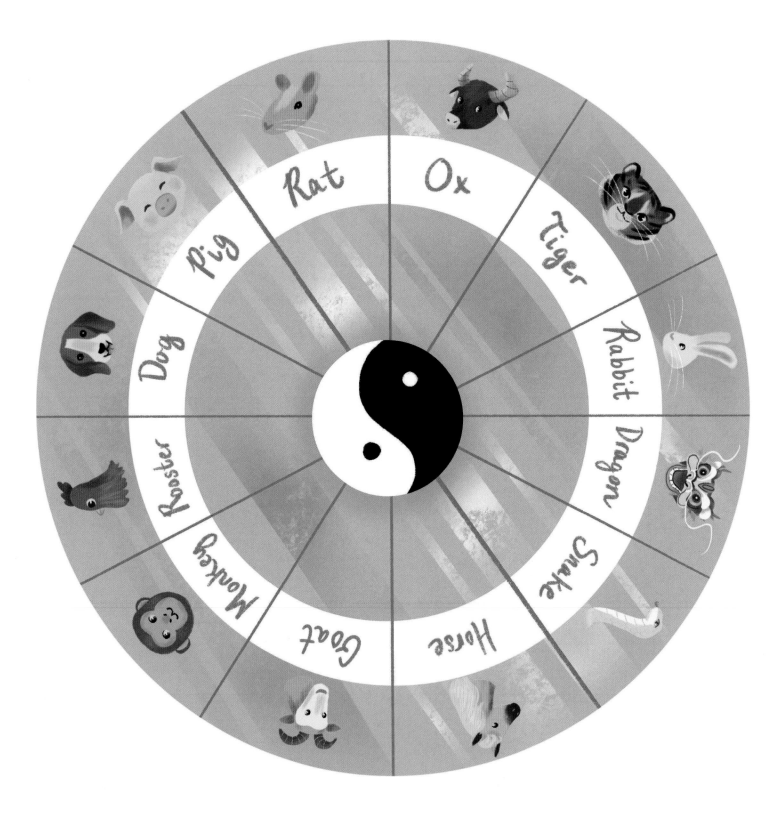

Each animal has a different personality—and the people born in the year of that animal are thought to have that personality. Which animal are you?

Rat

Clever
Charming
Wise

Ox

Gentle
Patient
Hardworking

Tiger

Brave
Playful
Generous

Rabbit

Shy
Kind
Artistic

Dragon

Proud
Generous
Smart

Snake

Clever
Curious
Graceful

Horse

Cheerful
Independent
Talkative

Goat

Easygoing
Gentle
Artistic

Monkey

Smart
Optimistic
Entertaining

Rooster

Funny
Neat
Adventurous

Dog

Loyal
Helpful
Trustworthy

Pig

Caring
Honest
Strong

Time to clean! In China, the tradition is to clean the house at least two days before the Lunar New Year. This is meant to sweep away any bad luck and wish for a fresh new year.

The color red is very important. It symbolizes luck and success. For the Lunar New Year, people wear red clothing and hang red decorations. Adults give children red envelopes filled with lucky money.

The red envelope is called hongbao in Mandarin. It is usually filled with crisp, new bills that bring happiness, health, and good luck. But be sure to receive the hongbao with both hands—using just one is considered rude.

Special red decorations are hung on doors of houses. They're meant to bring good luck and a peaceful new year to the family that lives there.

Time to eat! Lots of delicious foods are shared beginning on the eve of Lunar New Year. People eat dumplings, which represent a wealthy life. They eat fish, which represents a life full of all good things.

And they eat long noodles, which represent a long life.

Oranges are a popular Lunar New Year gift.
They are believed to bring good luck.

Legend has it that long ago, a beast with sharp teeth and horns would come to villages and eat people and livestock on the last day of Lunar New Year. Villagers discovered that hanging red lanterns and the noise the burning bamboo made scared the beast away.

Today, the Lantern Festival is celebrated on the last day of the Lunar New Year celebrations. People hang glowing lanterns in their homes and light firecrackers to scare away evil spirits.

POP!

And there are exciting parades—you may even see a colorful dragon or a dancing lion! Everyone makes noise with drums, cymbals, and gongs to frighten away evil spirits, bring good luck, and welcome the new year.

Happy Lunar New Year!